Now or Never:

Unraveling the Art of the Elusive Present

Now or Never:
Unraveling the Art of the Elusive Present

Table Of Contents

Introduction

Oh, yes, the present now! That elusive, playful sprite which always seems to slip through our fingers just as we think we've got it. If the present moment were a character in a novel, it would be that enigmatic figure everyone is looking for, a cross between Carmen Sandiego and Waldo. So, where in the world is it?

Let's start with the fundamentals. The "now" is that sliver of time between remembering that humiliating thing you did at the office party three years ago and thinking about that dental visit next week. That's the one.

The moment that somehow always gets overshadowed by its noisy neighbors, the

Past and the Future. Don't they two enjoy hogging the spotlight?

But let's be honest. It's not all their fault. Our brain is structured to recall and learn from the past while also planning and anticipating the future, thanks to its neuronal pathways. It's natural, sweetie! Our forefathers would not have survived if they were always in the 'present,' enjoying the gorgeous flowers without thinking about where they last saw a lion or where their next meal would come from.

However, while this skill was probably essential for avoiding being eaten on the prehistoric savannah, it may be the misery of our modern existence, especially when it causes us to miss out on the beauty and possibilities of the present.

If we had a penny for every time someone said, "live in the moment," I'm sure we'd all be sitting on our individual islands, sipping our favorite drink. And, while it may sound like a catchy bumper sticker, living in the moment is actually quite innovative.

This isn't just another manifesto encouraging you to "stop and smell the roses," though when was the last time you did that? It's a call to arms, or maybe a call to 'quiet'. A cry to recover the fleeting moment that, ironically, is all we truly have. That's how time works, which explains why sometimes if you do not act 'now', you may 'never' do it!

Have you ever had a day where you're physically there in a place - say, at a dinner table with pals - but your mind is elsewhere? Perhaps you're rehashing an old dispute or worrying about a work deadline. Meanwhile, the laughter, the taste of the food, and the pleasure of company all fade into the background, like an out-of-focus photograph. Everyone has been there. And we've all kicked ourselves later for losing out on life's true delights.

But here's a morsel of knowledge wrapped in a joke: Why didn't the mindfulness practitioner want to play hide and seek? Because it's difficult to hide when you're always in the present!

All kidding aside, "Now or Never: Unraveling the Art of the Elusive Present" is a guide to help you get out of the quicksand of "then" and "soon" and into the "here and now." This book intends to provide you with more than simply a passing acquaintance with the present time. We want a full-fledged romance, a whirlwind love affair with the present. It's doing it "now or never"!

We want to have transformed you into a master of the present, a connoisseur of the current, a... well, you get the picture.

In the following chapters, we'll delve deep into what it means to be present, why it's so difficult, and how we can teach our minds to accept the moment with a dash of humor and a dollop of patience.

So, if you're up for a voyage with more "aha!" moments than a detective thriller and less regrets than a questionable tattoo, keep reading.

And keep in mind that there is no time like the present. Literally.

Chapter 1:
Understanding the Now

Ever tried catching a drop of water with a sieve? Challenging, isn't it? Life often feels like that, especially when we attempt to grasp the idea of the present moment. We're surrounded by countless moments, but they seem to slip through our fingers just as swiftly as that elusive water drop.

But don't fret; you won't need waterproof clothing for this exploration. Instead, buckle up, as we embark on an exhilarating journey into the heart of time's greatest paradox. We're not just delving into any ordinary concept; we're tackling the grand master of them all - the ever-mystical "now." And trust me, by the time we're through, it's going to feel a lot more tangible than our water-drop conundrum.

So, what about the "now"? Some say it's omnipresent; others believe it's as mythical as a unicorn playing a ukulele. Whether you've mulled over it during a deep philosophical chat or simply in those quiet moments right before sleep, one thing's for certain: its allure is undeniable.

But what makes it so magnetic, so enigmatic? Let's embark on this quest to unwrap the layers of the present, one tick at a time.

Definition of "The Now"

Let's start with a little experiment. Pause for a moment and ask yourself, "What time is it?" If you glanced at your watch or smartphone, you missed the point. The answer is always the same: it's now.

Funny how we always seem to forget that, right?

At its simplest, the "now" is a point in time sandwiched snugly between the memory-laden past and the unpredictable future. You could imagine it as the creamy filling of an Oreo - the only part we're really interested in, but often overshadowed by the cookie parts. It's the only moment we truly experience firsthand, yet it's as elusive as a ninja cat on roller skates.

The Philosophical and Historical Context of Living in the Present

The fascination with the present isn't some hipster trend, like avocado toast or mismatched socks. This profound concept has deep historical roots. Heck, even before Socrates could question, "Why am I here?" (*probably waiting for his latte*), many were pondering the enigma of the present.

Take our pal Heraclitus from Ancient Greece. He mused, "You cannot step into the same river twice." But did he mean we need more river options, like a holiday brochure? Not quite. He was hinting at life's constant state of change, suggesting our moments are always fresh off the grill.

Across the seas, Eastern philosophies like Buddhism talked about life's impermanence, emphasizing that dwelling on that embarrassing high school dance move or daydreaming about your future self (*with a hopefully better dance repertoire*) causes us to miss life's concert while we're stuck adjusting the earphones.

And who could forget the serenity-promising Taoism? The "Tao Te Ching" basically nudged readers to chill and go with the flow. It's the ancient equivalent of "keep calm and carry on", minus the overpriced merchandise.

Not to be left out, literature got in on the action. From Rumi's poetic nudges to Thoreau's Walden winks, they sang praises of the now, making us wonder if they were perhaps the original mindfulness influencers.

Modern Science and Mindfulness

Zooming into the present (*pun intended!*), modern science, with all its gadgets and gizmos, found something spellbinding. It turns out, our sage-like predecessors were onto something. Who knew, right?

Neuroscience today offers insights previously relegated to the world of magic and midsummer night's dreams. It's now clear that practicing mindfulness isn't just a fancy way to show off at parties. It can actually rewire our brain! Engaging in the now can carve neural pathways that make you sharper, empathetic, and emotionally stable. So, while you might not get that Hogwarts letter, with a little mindfulness, you can still work some magic of your own.

Beyond the brain, psychologists have had their say. Research shows mindful folks experience less stress. So, while the rest of the world is busy losing its marbles over the WiFi signal, they're sipping tea, enjoying the chirp of a bird, or the meme their friend just shared.

And, just when you thought things couldn't get wackier, quantum physics joins the party. It throws ideas that sound like they're straight out of a sci-fi movie. Essentially, the act of observing, right in the present, might just play a role in shaping reality.

So, the next time you look at a cake and it seems to beckon, "Eat me!" – well, in a quantum world, maybe you just made it more delicious by the sheer act of observing. No guarantees, though!

As we roll this chapter to a close, what's the takeaway? The "now", often chased but seldom caught, isn't just a philosophical musing or a scientific hypothesis. It's the epicenter of life's great dance. And if you've ever tried dancing while focusing on your left foot, then your right, then that mysterious third one that shows up, you know how important it is to lose yourself in the rhythm of the moment.

So, lace up those dancing shoes. The great dance of "Now or Never: Unraveling the Art of the Elusive Present" has just begun, and guess what? It promises to be both enlightening and a barrel of laughs. See you on the dance floor! Or, you know, in the next chapter.

Chapter 2:
The Perils of Living Elsewhere

Ever been on one of those disastrous vacations where you think you're headed to a sunny beach, but you wind up in a swamp filled with mosquitoes?

Well, the journey of our minds isn't much different. While we aim for the serene shores of "Now," we often get sidetracked to the boggy marshlands of "What Was" and "What If". And let's face it, nobody likes unexpected swamp tours, especially without bug spray!

For all of humanity's evolution, our minds still behave like toddlers in a candy store. We're easily tempted by the shiny wrappers of the past and the promise of future treats. The present? It often ends up like that plain-looking, healthy snack that we ignore.

But it's time to flip the narrative and embrace the wholesome goodness of the present moment. Before that, let's embark on a brief detour through the candy aisles (*or, let's be honest, the trap-laden aisles*) of the Past and Future.

The Illusion of Past and Future

"Once upon a time..." Almost every captivating story begins with a look back. Ah, the past! It's like that high school sweetheart we never quite get over, no matter how many fish there are in the sea.

But here's the kicker: while it may be filled with nostalgia, victories, and lessons, it can also be a quagmire of what could've been. Conversely, the future is that dream date we haven't yet met but can't stop fantasizing about.

The allure of what lies ahead can be so intoxicating that we might start living there full-time. But as many sci-fi movies have shown us (*with the comical hairstyles and questionable fashion choices*), the future is unpredictable.

It's essential to recognize that both the past and future are, in many ways, illusions. The past is a tapestry of memories, and while they might feel vivid, they're not tangible or changeable.

The future, on the other hand, is merely a projection, as uncertain as next year's top TikTok dance trend. Will it be the robot? The moonwalk? Only time will tell.

How Anxiety, Regret, and Fear Steal the Present

Our brains, bless their squishy selves, have a flair for drama. When they're not reminiscing about that embarrassing slip in the cafeteria in 9th grade (*why, brain, why?!*), they're busy conjuring up scenarios where we're the star of our own disaster movie.

Anxiety is the brain's sneaky way of playing out worst-case future scenarios. Instead of focusing on the peaceful lunch right in front of us, we're mentally fighting off imaginary lions or preparing Oscar-winning speeches for mistakes we haven't even made yet.

Then there's regret, the past's signature perfume — scented with "I should've" and "If only I had". One whiff and we're transported to moments we wish played out differently. From missed opportunities to questionable karaoke song choices, our past can be a goldmine of cringe.

Fear, the third accomplice, straddles both past and future. It reminds us of past pains while simultaneously cautioning us against potential future ones, effectively double-teaming us out of the joy of the present. It's like being caught between two overzealous salespeople when all you wanted was to window shop.

The Health Implications of Not Being Present

Constantly time-traveling between the past and future is not only intellectually exhausting, but also a health risk. Unfortunately, it does not include any frequent flyer miles.

Studies have consistently demonstrated that being absent can cause an increase in cortisol levels, the body's major stress hormone. While a little tension can be just what we need to get started on that looming assignment (*or to flee when we see a bear*), persistent stress can be detrimental to our health.

Digestive problems, sleep disturbances, and even cardiovascular issues can arise when we're perpetually on this mental roller coaster. It's like our body's way of saying, "Hey, mind, cut it out! I'm trying to digest this taco, and your time-travel escapades aren't helping!"

Moreover, there's ample evidence to suggest that constant rumination can pave the way for more serious mental health issues, such as anxiety disorders and depression. Our minds, it turns out, really like stability. They're like that one friend who, after one merry-go-round ride, says, "I think I'll sit this one out."

As we wrap up our cautionary tour, it's evident that while occasional visits to the past and speculative trips to the future can offer insights, setting up permanent residence there isn't advisable. It's like overindulging in candy: a piece or two can be delightful, but too much and you're heading for a tummy ache.

As we journey further in "Now or Never: Unraveling the Art of the Elusive Present," we'll arm ourselves with tools to stay rooted in the now, making the most of every delicious, present moment. Safe travels, fellow time-traveler!

Chapter 3:
Techniques to Anchor in the Present

You know those intense workout DVDs that promise ripped abs and chiseled arms in just 10 minutes a day? Well, diving into the present isn't that much different (*minus the sweat and overly enthusiastic instructors*). The tools we need are always with us; it's just a matter of knowing how to use them.

Think of this chapter as your gym for the mind. We're about to embark on a mental fitness regime that'll make your consciousness feel like it's just run a mindfulness marathon. And don't worry, no heavy lifting is involved — unless you count lifting your spirits! Ready to flex those present-moment muscles?

Now, before we jump into the deep end of the now, it's good to remember that these techniques, like any form of exercise, get easier and more effective over time. It's not about perfection; it's about practice. The trick is consistency and a willingness to, occasionally, look a bit silly. (*Because let's face it, fully immersing oneself in the scent of a rose or the texture of a carpet can invite some curious glances.*)

Breathwork: The Natural Anchor

Breathing. It's something we all do, right? It's like the Wi-Fi of life – omnipresent but only truly appreciated when it's gone. (*Ever tried holding your breath and counting? Things get real, real fast!*) Yet, this basic life function serves as one of the most effective anchors to the present.

Our breath is always with us, unaffected by external events or our hectic schedules. We don't need to download an app, subscribe to a service, or even find a plug point. Breathwork, or conscious breathing, teaches us to focus on this natural rhythm, turning our attention inward and centering us in the present moment.

Test it out! Inhale deeply, hold for a few seconds, and then gently exhale. Feel the sensation of breath entering your lungs and your chest gently rising and falling. The portability of this technology is its beauty.

Are you stuck in traffic? Breathe. Do you have to wait for your computer to update? Breathe. Have you ever unintentionally viewed a scary film before going to bed? Definitely take a deep breath.

Grounding Exercises

Ever had one of those days where your mind feels like it's in a different time zone? Grounding exercises are like your mind's GPS, bringing you back to your current coordinates.

One popular method is the "5-4-3-2-1" technique. Here's how it works:

1. Identify 5 things you can see around you. Maybe it's the humorously oversized mug on your desk or that sock that's been missing its pair for weeks.

2. Acknowledge 4 things you can touch. Feel the fabric of your clothes, the smooth surface of your table, the warmth of your coffee mug, or even the cool touch of a windowpane.

3. Tune in to 3 things you can hear. The distant sound of traffic, birds chirping, or

the subtle hum of your refrigerator plotting world domination.

4. Note 2 things you can smell. Freshly brewed coffee? The scent of your favorite book? Or perhaps the suspicious smell of someone microwaving fish in the office kitchen.

5. Focus on 1 thing you can taste. This could be the lingering flavor from your last meal or even the taste of fresh air.

Voila! With each step, you're gently nudged back into the present. Think of it as a mini-vacation for the mind without the travel expenses.

Sensory Awareness Techniques

While we're on the topic of senses, let's dive deeper into them. The world is a symphony of experiences waiting to be felt. Sensory awareness techniques invite us to fully immerse ourselves in the moment, using our senses as a conduit to the now.

Take eating, for example. Ever tried savoring a piece of chocolate with your full attention? Feeling its texture, noting its aroma, and then letting it melt slowly in your mouth. It's not just eating; it's an experience.

The same goes for listening to music. Close your eyes and let each note, each rhythm, each lyric wash over you. Become one with the sound. It's like a private concert where you're the VIP, minus the ticket cost.

By tuning in to our senses and genuinely experiencing the world around us, not only can we anchor ourselves in the present, but also amplify our enjoyment of everyday moments. It's like upgrading life from standard definition to 4K ultra HD.

As we wrap up our training session in the gym of now, remember: the present moment is a gift (*pun intended!*). These techniques are merely tools in our mindfulness toolkit. The more you use them, the easier it becomes to unwrap the present, layer by layer, until every moment feels like a special occasion. So go ahead, give it a whirl and revel in the wonders of this "Now or Never Guide". And remember, no gym membership required!

Chapter 4:
Mindfulness Meditation

If you ever felt that the world is like a never-ending circus, with each of us juggling jobs, families, personal lives, and that ever-looming existential crisis, then you're not alone. But what if there was a backstage pass — a way to take a break from all the chaos and find a quiet corner to just...breathe?

That's where mindfulness meditation comes in. Think of it as your VIP ticket to the most exclusive show in town, where the only act is your own thoughts and the only sound, the rhythmic beating of your heart. Before we usher you to your seat in this serene auditorium of the mind, let's set the stage, shall we?

Mindfulness isn't just a trendy buzzword used by yoga enthusiasts or your friend who's taken a sudden liking to incense sticks and chakra-aligning crystals. It's an ancient practice that's as timeless as that one joke about meditation — "Don't hate, meditate!" Let's delve deeper, shall we?

Introduction to Mindfulness

Mindfulness. No, it's not about how full your mind is with to-do lists, random facts, or the lyrics to that one 90s song you can't get out of your head. It's about being fully present, fully engaged in whatever you're doing, without judgment or distraction. It's the anti-multitasking, the kryptonite to the wandering mind.

Mindfulness, which originated in Buddhist traditions, is like the wise old sage of meditation techniques, training us to watch our thoughts and feelings without becoming engrossed in them.

If our thoughts were clouds, mindfulness would be the bright, clear patch of sky between them, reminding us that calm is always available, even in the midst of life's storms.

Starting a Practice: A Step-by-Step Guide

Setting the Scene:
To cultivate mindfulness, you don't need a mountaintop, a Zen garden, or the droning chants of monks. A calm area of your home or a park bench will suffice. Simply pick a place where you can sit quietly for a bit.

Posture is important:
Sit comfortably. There's no need to imitate that lotus stance you saw on Instagram unless that's your thing. A simple chair can do miracles. Maintain a

straight back and hands on your lap. Feel regal, as if you're preparing to issue a royal proclamation.

Breathe Easy:
Concentrate on your breathing. Take note of the cool air entering your nostrils and the somewhat warmer air exhaling. You are the audience in a movie about your breath. There will be no reviews, only observations.

Allow Thoughts to Float:
Thoughts will come, just like those pesky door-to-door salespeople. Answer the door and reject them politely and let them go. There's no need to invite them around for tea.

Set a timer:
Set a timer for 5 minutes per day to begin. You can increase the time as you progress. But keep in mind that quality trumps quantity. A focused 5 minutes can

be more beneficial than an hour of distraction.

End on a high note:
When your timer goes off, slowly open your eyes. Move your fingers and toes as if you were meeting an old acquaintance, and gently reintroduce yourself to the world.

Common Challenges and Tips for Overcoming Them

Distractions, Distractions:
From the neighbor's wailing cat to the sudden urge to check if penguins have knees (they do), distractions abound.

Tip: Gently redirect your attention back to your breath. Every time you do this, consider it a mental push-up.

The Numbness Saga:

Sitting in one position might cause some tingling or numbness.

Tip: Adjust your posture slightly. Mindfulness is about comfort, not enduring pins and needles unless you're into that sort of thing.

I'm Bored!:

Yes, the mind can sometimes feel like a child on a long car ride.

Tip: Remember, the aim is to observe without judgment. Even boredom can be interesting if observed closely. It's like watching paint dry, but in a cool, introspective way.

Mindfulness meditation, in essence, is an intimate rendezvous with the present. It's your personal "pause" button in a world that's perpetually in fast-forward. As you advance in your "Now or Never" journey, may this practice become a sanctuary, a haven of serenity amidst the hustle and bustle.

And remember, if you ever get frustrated, just follow the ancient Zen saying: "If you can't find the sunshine, be the sunshine." Or was that a meme? Either way, happy meditating!

Chapter 5:
Beyond Meditation - Mindful Living

Ever heard of the phrase, "Don't just do something, stand there!"? No? Well, you might've if Yoda decided to be a mindfulness coach instead of a Jedi master. In the world of mindful living, that adage gets a twist.

Here, it's all about being present in what you're doing, rather than just breezing through tasks with your mind elsewhere. As the aficionado of our little guide, it's time to take the essence of mindfulness and sprinkle it over your day, like that extra bit of cheese you sneak onto your pizza when no one's looking.

Mindful living isn't just a monk-ish concept where you're perpetually draped in robes and spouting wise words. It's about transforming the mundane into the magical, making folding laundry feel like sculpting clay, and making eating a sandwich akin to tasting ambrosia. Get ready to make your ordinary day extraordinary.

Incorporating Mindfulness in Daily Tasks

It's all too easy to operate on autopilot. We've all been there: You drive home and can't quite remember the journey, or you brush your teeth while planning the next day in your head. By the time you rinse and spit, you've strategized an entire corporate takeover. But imagine how much richer our experiences would be if we truly engaged with them!

Showering Mindfully: Instead of mentally rehearsing that conversation you're dreading, feel the water on your skin. Observe the temperature, the sensation of droplets trickling down. Relish in the aroma of your shampoo or body wash. It's your own personal spa session, every day!

Mindful Cleaning: No, this isn't about cleaning your mind (*although that's a bonus*). It's about truly being present while cleaning. Feel the texture of the cloth, the motion of sweeping, and the transformation of a space from cluttered to clear. Who knew cleaning could be so... therapeutic?

Digital Mindfulness: When was the last time you checked your phone or scrolled social media and truly engaged? Try setting aside specific times to check notifications and fully engage with content rather than mindlessly scrolling. Your cat video viewing experience will elevate to cinematic proportions!

Mindfulness in the Acts of Eating, Walking, and Talking

Savor every mouthful of your food instead of gobbling it down like a contestant on a reality show; this is one way to practice mindful eating. Take note of the different flavors, scents, and textures. Consuming a raisin may take as little as five minutes, giving you a delectable bite-sized gourmet adventure.

Mindful Walking: This isn't about walking and simultaneously trying not to step on a crack (*though that could be fun*). Feel each step, the ground beneath your feet, and the rhythm of your stride. Nature walks take on a whole new meaning when you're truly present.

Mindful Speaking: Remember the last time you blurted something out and immediately wished for a rewind button? We've all been there. Mindful speaking involves truly listening, considering your words, and speaking from a place of authenticity and kindness. It's less about a filter and more about intention.

Creating Mindful Spaces at Home and Work

Having a dedicated space for mindfulness, whether it's a corner of your room with a meditation cushion or a spot on your office desk with a calming plant, can act as a beacon for your mindful practices.

Mindful Corners: Designate a little nook at home where everything is about the present. Maybe it's a chair with a soft throw, a small table with a calming candle, and your favorite book. This is your recharge zone.

Desk Zen: Transform a portion of your work desk into a mindful oasis. A few succulents, a mini fountain, or even calming desk toys can become tools of relaxation amidst the chaos of deadlines and emails.

Mindful Reminders: Place sticky notes with mindful cues around your living or workspace. A simple "Breathe" or "Stay Present" can pull you back from the rabbit hole of overthinking.

So, there you have it! From the way you munch on your morning toast to how you curate your surroundings, every moment offers an opportunity to be truly, madly, deeply in the 'now'. As you go about your day, remember our mantra from this guide.

Each activity, no matter how seemingly trivial, can be a gateway to presence. And if you ever feel yourself drifting into autopilot, just whisper to yourself, "It's now or never." Or sing it, if you're in a mood for a little Bon Jovi! Cheers to the art of the present!

Chapter 6: Overcoming Distractions and Challenges

Okay, intrepid reader. Imagine you've just decided to take a moment for yourself, perhaps to meditate or just enjoy a hot cup of tea in peace. You're settling in, feeling the serene ambiance. And just as you're about to relish the silence... ding! Your phone announces the arrival of yet another cat meme in the group chat. Or your brain helpfully reminds you of that one embarrassing thing you did a decade ago.

Welcome to the gladiatorial arena of the present moment, where our modern-day life throws lions, tigers, and, well, notifications at us. So what should we do?

Now let's face the common adversaries of the here and now with a mix of strategies, wisdom, and a splash of humor.

Recognizing and Mitigating External Distractions

Ah, external distractions. They're like that one friend who can't help but photobomb every single picture. Except in life, they're photobombing your peaceful moments.

Technology Tyrants: Smartphones, tablets, and smart-everything-else are amazing tools. But they can quickly become dictators of our attention. Consider setting specific "tech-free" times during your day. Turn off non-essential notifications or even have short device detox periods. Remember the good old times when we looked up to see the sky and not just another notification?

Ambient Anarchists: This includes the neighbor's yappy dog, the perpetual road construction, or the unexpected doorbell. While you can't control all of these, noise-canceling headphones or white noise machines can be life (*and peace*) savers.

People Puzzles: Ever tried to have a mindful moment and someone decides it's the best time to discuss the weather, existential crises, or the latest TV show plot twist? Politely communicate your need for some undisturbed time or set specific "me-time" slots.

The Inner Critic and How to Tame It

The inner critic. A voice that's often more nagging than a room full of disgruntled seagulls. It's that voice that says you're not doing 'mindfulness' right or dredges up cringy memories from 2009.

Acknowledgment, Not Argument: Recognize the voice for what it is - just a voice, not the entirety of you. Instead of arguing, simply acknowledge its presence. "Oh hey, critic. Fancy meeting you here in my psyche, AGAIN."

Compassionate Conversation: Instead of berating yourself, try a little tenderness. Speak to yourself as you would a dear friend. Replace "Why can't I focus?" with "It's okay. Let's try again."

Visualization: Imagine the critic as a character. Maybe it's a grumpy old librarian or a cartoonish villain. By giving it a persona, you can differentiate it from your true self and even chuckle at its antics.

Establishing Boundaries for a Present-focused Life

Living in the now is like trying to build a sandcastle while waves (*or distractions*) constantly erode it. Here's how to construct a protective moat.

Time Blocking: Allocate specific chunks of time for tasks. When it's relaxation time, fully relax. When it's work, be all in. It creates a rhythm and structure, preventing bleed-over of distractions.

Mindful Communication: Share your journey of being in the 'now' with close ones. They'll understand and respect your boundaries better. Plus, who knows? They might join you in the quest for the elusive present!

Environmental Enhancements: Curate your surroundings. Maybe a "Do Not Disturb" sign or a calming workspace filled with plants. Create an environment that supports, not sabotages, your intentions.

So, the next time your phone buzzes with that tempting allure of a viral video or your inner critic tries to gatecrash your tranquility party, you'll be ready. Equip yourself with the strategies from this guide and smile in the face of distractions.

Because when it comes to embracing the 'now', the time is, you guessed it, now or never! And just between us, you've got this. Go forth and conquer the present, you mindful maverick!

Chapter 7:
The Role of Technology

Let's embark on a brief time-travel experiment. Imagine a day in the life of our ancestors, say, 10,000 years ago. Their to-do list might have looked something like: "Hunt. Gather. Avoid saber-toothed tigers."

Fast forward to today, and our modern-day list goes: "Check emails. Scroll through social media. Avoid spoilers for the latest binge-worthy show." Quite the evolution, right? And it's not just our to-do lists that have evolved, but the very way we experience the world.

We live in an age where we can connect with someone on the other side of the planet with a tap, but sometimes we end up feeling more disconnected than ever from the world around us and our inner selves. Navigating the digital labyrinth without losing yourself is a modern-day art, an art of balance, boundaries, and, occasionally, chuckling at autocorrect fails.

How Modern Tech Competes for Our Attention

Remember when phones were just, well, phones? Now, they're our alarm clocks, cameras, music players, and personal assistants rolled into one. It's like they attended a 'Jack of All Trades' convention and came back overly enthusiastic.

The Instant Gratification Game: With every like, share, and retweet, our brain releases a feel-good chemical called dopamine. It's the same pleasure-reward system that our ancestors experienced after a successful hunt, but instead of mammoths, we're hunting for memes.

Notification Nation: Each ping and pop-up is designed to draw our attention. It's like having a persistent child tugging at your sleeve every few minutes. "Look at me! Look at me!"

Endless Scroll Syndrome: Whether it's social media, news sites, or streaming platforms, the 'infinite scroll' or 'next episode auto-play' features trap us in a loop. It's the digital version of "Just one more chip"... until the bag is empty, except in this case, the bag never seems to be empty!

Tips for a Mindful Relationship with Technology

So, how do we dance with technology without stepping on each other's toes?

Intention Over Impulse: Before diving into the digital realm, ask yourself, "Why am I reaching for my device?" Is it out of boredom, habit, or genuine need?

Quality Over Quantity: Aim for meaningful online interactions. Comment genuinely on a friend's post or engage in a thoughtful discussion. Remember, it's not about how many friends you have, but the quality of friendships.

Tech-Free Times: Designate specific hours or even whole days when you're not beholden to the beck and call of your device. It might be the time post-dinner or the entire Sunday. Find what suits you.

Digital Detox: How and Why

"Digital Detox". It sounds like a fancy spa treatment where your devices get cucumber slices over their screens.

The Science Behind It: Continuous exposure to screens can mess with our sleep cycles, strain our eyes, and even add to our stress. A detox lets our brains recharge, improving concentration, sleep quality, and overall mental well-being.

Starting Small: You don't need to go cold turkey. Start by reducing screen time in small increments. Maybe stop screen time half-hour before bed or avoid looking at your devices during meals.

Beyond Screens: This is your chance to reacquaint yourself with offline pleasures. Read a physical book, go for a walk, or even try your hand at doodling or journaling.

Our relationship with technology is a bit like indulging in chocolate cake. A slice here and there? Blissful. But overindulge, and you might feel a tad queasy. Remember, in the dance of life, you lead, and technology follows. Or in tech-speak, let's ensure our Wi-Fi connections never come at the cost of our inner connection. Cheers to syncing with the 'now', one digital step at a time!

Chapter 8: The Benefits of Living in the Now

In the grand theater of life, where past regrets and future anxieties often steal the limelight, there exists an unsung hero – the present moment. It's like the understudy that has been waiting in the wings forever, only to dazzle the audience when finally given a chance.

You see, while the 'now' doesn't come with flashy laser lights or a dramatic soundtrack, it has a magic all its own. That magic, dear reader, brings with it a plethora of benefits, or as I like to think of them, the "golden tickets" to a wholesome life. And no, you don't need to wrestle them from the hands of Willy Wonka. You just have to be, well, here. Right now. Let's unwrap these golden tickets and see what treasures they hold, shall we?

Enhanced Mental Well-being

"Why did I say that in the meeting?" "What will happen if I don't meet the deadline?" We've all been trapped in this mental ping-pong match between past mistakes and future fears. But when you anchor yourself in the present, you give your mind a much-needed break from this endless rally.

Peace and Calm: Just like you wouldn't run your car non-stop without breaks, living in the present gives your mind its well-deserved pit stops. The result? Reduced mental fatigue and a general feeling of lightness. Kind of like mental yoga!

Clarity of Thought: Imagine trying to watch TV with 20 other channels playing in the background. Confusing, right? Being present declutters your mind, providing clear reception to just one channel – the present. Farewell, mental static!

Resilience to Stress: When you live in the now, problems are just situations waiting for solutions, not catastrophic events. It's the difference between navigating a maze with enthusiasm versus being lost in a doom-filled labyrinth.

Improved Physical Health and Longevity

Turns out, the mind and body aren't just best friends; they're inseparable twins. What affects one, invariably impacts the other. By cozying up to the present moment, your body reaps some surprising rewards.

A Heart at Peace: Chronic stress, the pesky consequence of not living in the now, is notorious for raising blood pressure and heart risks. Embracing the present serves as a natural pacifier for your ticker.

Boosted Immunity: Who needs a superhero shield when living in the moment naturally bolsters your defense against illnesses? Stress hormones can suppress the immune system, but a present-focused approach gives those defenses a leg up.

A Longer, More Vibrant Life: There's evidence to suggest that mindfulness and present-moment awareness can extend lifespan. It's like your cells are throwing a little party every time you live in the now, celebrating with better health and longevity.

Deepened Relationships and Social Connections

Ever spoken to someone who's physically present but miles away mentally? Not the most satisfying chat, right? Being present isn't just a solo gig; it's a harmonious duet with everyone around you.

Genuine Listening: By being in the moment, you listen to respond, not just to react. It transforms everyday conversations into genuine connections. And before you know it, you've become the Oprah of your social circle.

Authentic Interactions: When you're genuinely present, your interactions aren't tainted by past grudges or future worries. They become pure, genuine, and straight from the heart. No need for emotional filters.

Increased Empathy and Understanding: Living in the now gives you the superpower of truly understanding others. You see them for who they are, not through the foggy lens of your biases.

The 'now' isn't just a time stamp on a clock or a fleeting moment on a timeline; it's the golden ticket to a life of richness, depth, and joy. From the tranquility of your mind to the vitality of your body, from the depths of your personal introspections to the heights of social connections, every corner of your existence gleams brighter in the light of the present.

So, the next time you find yourself adrift in the vast oceans of time, remember: the most rewarding shores are often right beneath your feet. Dive in!

Chapter 9:
Stories from the Present

Life, they say, is up made of moments. But for some, these moments stretch longer, richer, and more vibrant, painting their lives with a palette of colors most of us seldom see. Why? Because they chose to dance, not just live, in the present.

Imagine life's song playing its heart out, and these folks are grooving to every beat, while some of us are still fumbling with the volume buttons. Before we dive into their stories, let's touch upon the age-old question: "Where do you find such mystical, present-embracing beings?" Oh, you'll be surprised!

Finding Your 'Now' Tribe

While the journey of embracing the present is a deeply personal one, it's often illuminated by the tales, experiences, and wisdom of others who've treaded similar paths. Think of them as signposts, guiding you when the path seems unclear, or as fellow dancers, teaching you new moves in this dance of the 'now'.

Yet, like all precious things in life, these inspiring souls aren't always on prominent display. Sometimes, they're hidden in plain sight, waiting for you to take a moment, pause, and truly see. So, as you embark on this quest of finding your tribe, remember, it's not about seeking perfection but resonance.

You're not looking for flawless gurus but genuine souls who, through their ups and downs, have glimpsed the magic of the present. And as you meet them, you'll realize: the 'now' isn't a solitary space. It's a vibrant, collective celebration!

Tips to Find Inspiring People

Join Mindfulness Retreats or Workshops: While it might sound like a fantastical Hogwarts for the mindful, such retreats are very real and very beneficial. They attract folks who not only practice being in the present but have tales of transformation to share. And no, you don't have to chant spells, just mantras.

Engage in Online Mindfulness Forums and Groups: The internet isn't just about cute cat videos and memes. Online platforms can be havens for sharing and learning from real-life stories of people around the world. Who knew clicking could be so enlightening?

Attend Local Yoga or Meditation Classes: Often, these classes aren't just about flexing the body, but also the mind. And you'll likely meet individuals who are on similar quests, or better yet, have found what they were seeking in the embrace of the 'now'.

Read Biographies of Mindfulness Practitioners: Some tales are worth the paper they're printed on. Dive into life stories of renowned mindful personalities. Their journey, detailed in words, can be the compass you need.

Listen Actively in Day-to-Day Conversations: Inspiration isn't confined to seminars or books. Sometimes, it's hidden in everyday conversations with friends, family, or even a talkative Uber driver. So, next time someone's sharing, lend more than just an ear. You might catch a tale worth its weight in gold!

The Essence of Ordinary Miracles

In the hustle and bustle of life, there are moments that sparkle with an extraordinary light, not because they're grand or world-changing, but because someone chose to truly inhabit them.

These stories aren't of individuals scaling mountains or diving deep into the ocean's abyss. Instead, they are tales of ordinary people who, in a seemingly mundane moment, discovered the profound. They found beauty in the banal, depth in the daily, and wonder in the 'why not'.

As you read these narratives, let them serve as a gentle reminder that the door to the present moment often isn't guarded by grand gestures but by simple acts of mindful awareness. Sometimes, all it takes to touch eternity is to engage deeply with a fleeting second.

Welcome to the realm where every tick of the clock is an invitation to dive into the infinite ocean of now.

Inspirational Moments of Mindful Awareness

Here are some examples of people who have started to live a more fruitful life because they've found the way to living in the present!

Sarah's Symphony:
Sarah was a cellist, lost in the world of orchestras and compositions. One day, during a mundane practice session, she decided to truly "listen" to her cello. Not just hear, but listen. And for the first time, she didn't just play music; she felt it coursing through her, connecting her to that very moment. Today, Sarah doesn't just perform; she lives her performances.

Tom's Morning Brew:

Tom wasn't a monk or a philosopher. He was just a guy who loved his morning coffee. One day, instead of gulping it down, he sipped it slowly, savoring every flavor, every aroma. That coffee didn't just wake him up; it woke him up to the present. Now, Tom's mornings aren't just caffeinated; they're awakened.

Mia's Silent Walk:

Mia was an urban dweller, always rushing. One evening, amidst the chaos of the city, she chose to walk in silence, observing, feeling, and absorbing every little detail around her. The city, for the first time, revealed its silent tales and vibrant hues. Mia's walks aren't just exercises now; they're experiences.

In every corner, in every shadow, and sometimes, right in front of us, there are stories waiting to be discovered, tales of the magical present. All it takes is a bit of curiosity and the willingness to listen.

So, as you navigate your life, remember to occasionally stop, feel, and absorb the tales that the 'now' whispers in your ears. They might just be the fairytales you've been seeking!

Chapter 10:
Moving Forward Mindfully

You've journeyed with us through the valleys and peaks of the present moment, danced with the nuances of "now", and are probably wondering, "How do I keep this party going?"

Fret not, dear reader. The eternal conga line of life continues, and while we may have reached the final chapter of this book, your adventure with the "now" is just beginning.

After all, there's a reason it's called "Now or Never"! Time waits for no one, and neither should you! As you pack your bags and don your cap of mindful living, let's gear you up for the road ahead.

Continually Cultivating a Present-focused Mindset

The mind is like a garden; it thrives when tended to and can easily get overrun by weeds if neglected. But fear not, you won't be battling any triffids here. Instead, these are the more benign distractions of life that can pull us from the current moment.

By actively tending to our mental landscape, ensuring that we sow seeds of mindfulness and regularly weed out distractions, we can create a lush, present-focused mindset.

Daily Reflections: Begin or end your day with a moment of introspection. What were the moments when you felt most alive? When did you drift away? Recognizing these can help reinforce the former and reduce the latter.

Mindful Reminders: Set hourly chimes or place sticky notes in prominent places. These little nudges can be the jolt back to the present.

Curate Your Environment: Surround yourself with symbols, artwork, or quotes that remind you of the beauty of now. Sometimes, a little visual inspiration can go a long way.

Embracing Change and Uncertainty

Life, with its infinite wisdom, has a knack for throwing curveballs. Just when you think you've mastered the slide into home base, you find out you're actually on a rugby field. Oops!

Change and uncertainty are the only certainties in life. Embracing them doesn't mean enjoying every tumultuous moment, but it does mean accepting their inevitability.

Adopting a Beginner's Mind: Every situation, even if it's familiar, has something new to offer. By approaching it with fresh eyes, you'll be less caught up in past patterns.

Finding Grounding Rituals: Whether it's a specific breathing technique or a personal mantra, having a go-to practice can provide stability in shaky times.

Celebrate the Small Victories: It's not just about embracing big changes but cherishing the tiny shifts. Did you stay present during a stressful meeting? Win! Managed not to ruminate over that awkward conversation for more than ten minutes? Double win!

Lifelong Resources for Deepening the Practice

The journey to the "now" isn't a sprint; it's a marathon (*and not the Netflix kind, although being present during a binge-session can be a practice in itself!*). As you move forward, remember to continually nourish your practice.

Engage in Continuous Learning: The field of mindfulness is vast, with new research, insights, and techniques emerging regularly. Keep updated through books, workshops, or online courses.

Join a Community: Whether it's a local meditation group or an online forum, being part of a community can provide motivation, support, and new perspectives.

Seek Out Retreats: Sometimes, the best way to dive deep is to step back. Consider joining mindfulness retreats, which can offer immersive experiences to bolster your practice.

And there you have it — a toolkit for your voyage ahead. While the pages of this book may end, the story of your dance with the present is just getting started. Remember, in the grand theatre of life, every moment is a once-in-a-lifetime performance. So, why not make it count? After all, it's "Now or Never"!

Conclusion

Here we are, standing at the metaphorical train station, looking back at the tracks we've traveled, while feeling the electric anticipation for the routes yet to be discovered. As the final notes of our "Now or Never" symphony start to play, let's momentarily put on our nostalgic hats (and no, not those old fedoras you've stashed at the back of your closet).

Think of this not as a goodbye but as a grand "See you in the now!" moment. Let's toast to the "nows" we've explored and to the countless ones that await. Because, as a wise person once said, "It's not about the destination, but the journey... unless you're trying to find the restroom, then it's definitely the destination."

Recap of the Journey

We embarked on this voyage with a curious spirit, and my, what an expedition it's been! From unraveling the intricate tapestry of the "now" to navigating the digital jungles and their attention-snatching creatures, we've walked (*and sometimes danced*) our way through the art and science of mindful living.

We've peeked into stories that inspire, techniques that ground, and strategies to keep the pesky distractions at bay. With each page turned, we hoped to have deepened our collective understanding and appreciation of the present moment.

Personal Reflection and Commitment to the Practice

As we momentarily sit in the train's quiet compartment of reflection, think back to where you started. What has shifted within you? Perhaps there's a newfound tranquility, or maybe you've grown to befriend that cheeky inner critic.

This journey was personal, unique, and if we're being honest, hopefully sprinkled with moments of delightful surprise. But like any treasured habit, the true magic of mindfulness unfolds with consistent practice. It's like maintaining a spunky potted plant or a pet rock (*with fewer responsibilities and no watering required*).

An Invitation to Live Every Moment Fully

Consider this not an end, but a perpetual invitation — a standing RSVP — to revel in the abundance of each moment. Every tick of the clock, every rustling leaf, every spontaneous chuckle offers an open door to the grand ballroom of the present.

So, with the heart of an explorer and the enthusiasm of someone who's just discovered they had an extra piece of chocolate in their pocket, stride forth!

Here's to the countless "nows" that await, to the tales you'll weave, the memories you'll craft, and to the gift of the present. After all, dear reader, remember: it's "Now or Never"! And, between you and me, "now" sounds like a fantastic choice! Cheers!

Appendices

Well, well, well! If you've made it to the Appendices, then hats off to you! Or should we say, "mindful caps" to you?

It seems your appetite for diving deep into the world of the present moment is insatiable—and that's just the kind of enthusiasm we love to see. This section is like the extra whipped cream on your favorite dessert — something you didn't know you needed but will thoroughly relish.

Let's gear up for a treasure trove of tools, resources, and golden nuggets to supercharge your present-moment adventures.

Recommended Readings and Resources

So, you're hungry for more brain food, eh? Not to fear, dear bibliophile! Here's a curated list of books and resources that would make even the grumpiest librarian crack a smile:

"The Power of Now" by Eckhart Tolle - A classic dive into the essence of living in the present.

"Wherever You Go, There You Are" by Jon Kabat-Zinn - A delightful exploration into the beauty of the present, wherever you might find yourself.

"Radical Acceptance" by Tara Brach - For those moments when you feel like a squirrel caught in a traffic light's glare. Breathe, accept, and move forward.

Mindful.org - An online oasis brimming with articles, guided practices, and a community passionate about mindful living.

Local Mindfulness Workshops - Often, community centers or local spiritual groups offer courses and workshops on mindfulness. They're like gym sessions for your soul, minus the sweat!

Mindfulness Apps and Tools

In a digital world where there's an app for almost everything — including one to remind you to drink water (*because apparently, basic human survival instincts are so last century*) — why not leverage tech for mindfulness? Here are some stellar apps to anchor you:

Headspace - If meditation had a cozy digital living room, this would be it.

Calm - For those moments when life feels like a blender set on 'frappe', this app will soothe your senses.

Insight Timer - Boasting a huge library of guided meditations, it's like the Netflix of mindfulness. But don't binge too hard; we don't want you floating away!

Aura - Tailored meditation experiences based on your mood. Feeling grumpy? There's a meditation for that!

Guided Meditation Scripts

Ready to play tour guide for a journey within? These scripts are perfect for solo sessions or guiding a group. Just remember to speak with a voice that's calmer than a sloth on vacation:

The Breath's Embrace:

Begin by finding a comfortable seat. If you're on a spiky cactus, reconsider your choices. Close your eyes and take three deep breaths, inhaling the calm, exhaling the chaos. Visualize your breath as a gentle wave, washing over the shores of your being, cleansing and renewing.

Forest of Serenity:

Picture yourself standing at the edge of a tranquil forest. No, there are no WiFi signals here, but trust me, the connection is strong. With every step, feel the crunch of leaves, hear the symphony of nature, and immerse in the forest's embrace. Breathe in the forest's essence, exhale any lingering tension.

Remember, whether you're flipping through recommended readings or guiding a meditation, the journey into the present is always ripe with possibility. It's not about perfection but about embracing the fullness of every moment. Onward, brave traveler!

www.ingramcontent.com/pod-product-compliance
Lightning Source LLC
Chambersburg PA
CBHW061349140726
47997CB00003B/1122